From the o... m...!

C000183870

21/5/13

And I dreamt a marvellous dream:
I was in a wilderness, I could not tell where,
and looking Eastwards I saw a tower
high up against the sun, and splendidly
built on top of a hill...

PIERS THE PLOWMAN
William Langland

PREPOSTEROUS ERECTIONS

A BOOK OF ENGLISH TOWERS

Peter Ashley

F

FRANCES LINCOLN LIMITED
PUBLISHERS

Frances Lincoln Limited
www.franceslincoln.com

Preposterous Erections
Copyright © Frances Lincoln Limited 2012
Text and photographs copyright © Goldmark 2012

First Frances Lincoln edition 2012
Published in association with Goldmark

Book designed by Peter Ashley

All rights reserved.
No part of this publication may be reproduced, stored
in a retrieval system, or transmitted, in any form, or
by any means, electronic, mechanical, photocopying,
recording or otherwise without the prior written
permission of the publisher or a licence permitting
restricted copying. In the United Kingdom such licences
are issued by the Copyright Licensing Agency,
Saffron House, 6–10 Kirby Street, London EC1N 8TS.

A catalogue record for this book is
available from the British Library.

978-0-7112-3358-4

Printed and bound in China

1 2 3 4 5 6 7 8 9

Page 1: Gothic Temple, Stowe, Buckinghamshire

Page 2: Abberley Clock Tower, Worcestershire

Page 5: (opposite) Horton Tower, Dorset

Page 128: Old John, Leicestershire

Iste liber est dedicata a
Septem per Quinque

They can be the architecture of the isolated, the *momento mori* for uncontainable egos and, for those of us passing by below, the eye-catching stimulants of the imagination. Lord Berners, who painted his Faringdon tower that overlooks the landscape between Oxford and Swindon (opposite), also said that ideally they should be of no use at all. The word 'folly' is the label most often attached to them, and at least everyone immediately knows what's being talked about. But the word always has a tendency to suggest foolish and absurd actions, that these highly visible towers are somehow just fanciful whimsy. To our eyes, many perhaps are the results of the fevered imaginings of those wanting to leave their mark on country estates – one only has to think of William Beckford's Fonthill skyscraper demolishing itself on a Wiltshire hilltop – but it would be wrong to think of all their builders as profligate and unthinking meglomaniacs. However, as predominately an eighteenth-century pastime, folly building does indeed rise up into our consciousness with varying degrees of both idiosyncrasy and incongruity, and all are embued with a certain intrigue and curiosity. Not just as to purpose (or lack of it) but also to set us enquiring about who had these ideas in the first place, how much they cost to build, and what took place in and on such singular flights of fancy.

Preposterous Erections will take us out into the English counties, down the driveways of rural estates, up to the crests of dominant hills, and so into the minds and preoccupations of their initiators – be they monuments, would-be observatories, mausolea or just landscape eye-catchers. Not all will be the crowning ornaments first seen on distant hilltops; towers can equally arrive unexpectedly in our peripheral vision in a wood or down a country lane, and although the traditional idea of a folly tower is firmly embedded in the past, (Faringdon was said to be the last, until very recently), there are times when something extraordinary catches our eyes in the modern age, and we still exclaim 'What on earth is that?' Preposterous erections will always have the ability to amaze, puzzle, arouse and delight the curious and inquiring mind.

FRESTON TOWER, SUFFOLK

Out on the Shotley Peninsular south of Ipswich is Freston Tower, a remarkable red brick eyrie overlooking the Orwell Estuary. Usually recognised as the first English folly tower, Freston may nevertheless have started out as simply part of a large house built here in the mid-sixteenth century by either one of the Latymer family or, more likely, Sir Thomas Gooding, a wealthy Ipswich merchant who bought Freston Manor from them in 1553. The tower provided uninterrupted views of ships moving up to the quays and warehouses of Tudor Ipswich and, in our times, of white pleasure yachts moored at anchor on Freston Reach. There is also the thought that it was built as a viewing tower for Queen Elizabeth's progress up to Ipswich in 1561.

Of course all towers like this must have a more fanciful story, and the one here is that it was built as a series of study rooms for the education of Ellen de Freston, one on each of the six storeys. Each room is 12 feet by 10 feet, served by a staircase whose crenallated turret can be seen behind the parapet. We are not told what the subjects were, but apparently the little room at the very top was hung with tapestries, so probably this was where Ellen learnt carpet beating. Freston Tower is now in the care of the Landmark Trust, whose visitors' logbook states: 'We have enjoyed living vertically for a week – sad to be coming back down to earth'.

GOTHIC TEMPLE
STOWE, BUCKINGHAMSHIRE

When I first saw this gingerbread confection in a photograph, I really thought it must be some Victorian extravaganza, a garden pavilion for a Puginesque aesthete to entertain lady accolytes with his mezzotints. And that's because Stowe's Gothic Temple is a supreme example of very early gothic revival which, like much Victoriana, has its origins in medieval ecclesiastical building. But this is the 1740s, and James Gibbs contrasted the pale limestone used elsewhere on the Stowe estate by using a heavily ferruginous Northamptonshire ironstone. Triangular in plan, turrets, cupolas and pinnacles pierce the sky to give a magical silhouette against the sun, helped by its isolated position in the un-landscaped Hawkwell Field. Was an ancestor of the Scots pine there originally I wonder? Even if deliberately planted, this tree is an impressive natural foil to the gothic pilasters, castellated gables and quatrefoil window openings.

Cars parked discreetly round on the north side give a clue as to its current use. Although the Stowe landscaped gardens are administered by the National Trust, the Gothic Temple is a star in the inestimable Landmark Trust catalogue, which means that you and your friends can come and live in it for a week. What ghosts would entertain you here. A barely perceived hooded figure perhaps, standing under a Holm oak in the park, watching the Temple blinds being drawn against the last of the evening light.

BELMOUNT TOWER, LINCOLNSHIRE

Belton House and its parkland sits just to the north of Grantham.
Built between 1685-88 by Sir John Brownlow, the house is a superb
example of Carolean style with balustrades, a central cupola and the
latest fashion for sash windows. Out across the park from the east side of
the mansion an avenue of trees rises up towards the Lincolnshire Edge,
a narrow ridge running from Stamford to the Humber with a gap for
Lincoln. The avenue finishes, and there with its back against the woods
is the extraordinary Belmount Tower.

More archway than true tower, this is one of the architectural
additions made to the park by Brownlow's nephew Sir John Brownlow
III (later Viscount Tyrconnel) who inherited Belton in 1721. The
belvedere, or prospect tower, was completed in the 1750s and promptly
became affectionately known as 'Lord Brownlow's Trousers'. Originally
there were flanking pavilions, but the sides are now curiously buttressed
by stone and brickwork that extends almost to the wooden balustraded
roofline. Fifty-odd years ago the incumbent Lord Brownlow returned
from Jamaica to find these timbers ablaze. His astonishment is perhaps
reflected in the glazed round windows, Venetian window and gaping
archway making an architectural face.

I had to wait up here a considerable time for a decent amount of light,
and discovered that when lying down amongst thistles and grass, sheep
will come right up to you as they graze, scattering when you get up
again.

LORD COBHAM'S PILLAR
STOWE, BUCKINGHAMSHIRE

Stowe is unique in showing a complete range of eighteenth-century landscaping in a remarkable series of garden and parkland pavilions, grottoes, temples and rotundas. Here is a veritable theme park of 'follies', everything from a Temple of Concord and Victory that would be at home amongst cypresses on a Tuscan hillside, to a Palladian Bridge that seems to come straight out of the mould made for those at Wilton and Prior Park.

The wife of the 4th Baronet, Sir Richard Temple (1669-1749), had this stunning column designed by James Gibbs in the last two years of her husband's life. Lord Cobham's Pillar is, at 104 feet, the tallest of the Stowe monuments, and a fitting punctuation mark as it virtually concludes the main stage of garden building at Stowe. A spiral staircase winds up to the little glazed belvedere that in turn is surmounted by a statue of Lord Cobham in the almost obligatory Roman armour. High winds buffeting the column brought buttresses to the base in 1792, designed by Valdré, each sporting a Coade stone lion. The same lightning strike that toppled Lord Cobham from his perch in 1957 also put paid to three of the lions. All were replaced in a 2001 restoration.

DUNSTALL CASTLE, WORCESTERSHIRE

This curious eye-catcher of circa 1750 sits at the side of a common not far from Defford, just off the Pershore to Upton road. It forms part of a series of such things surrounding Croome Court that includes the Panorama and Pirton Castle, and is most likely attributable to Sanderson Miller working for the 6th Earl of Coventry. Robert Adam was here on the estate in the 1760s and is sometimes associated with it. Certainly it would come as no surprise to have Miller's name confirmed; the mid-eighteenth century saw him running around the Midland counties getting numerous erections off the ground before finally going bonkers.

Croome Court is to the north, and this *faux* Norman ruin would have made an impressive silhouette with its two tall arches. An equally tall hedge behind it lessens some of the impact now, but at least its 'at risk' status has been removed with extensive but sympathetic restoration by the National Trust in 2010.

MOW COP, CHESHIRE

This curious sham castle is only just in Cheshire, overlooking the Plain and a mossy stone's throw from Staffordshire. I first became aware of it when it was a key location in Alan Garner's book *Red Shift*, and again when I bought a copy of W.G. Hoskins' seminal *The Making of The English Landscape* where it was used dramatically on the front cover.

Ordinary streets of houses rise up and around the precipitous cone of rock, and then it is but a very short steep climb up to the tower itself, built as a summer house in 1754 for Randle Wilbraham to see from his newly-built house Rode Hall, three miles away in a Cheshire valley. It must have made an impressive silhouette against the dawn light, and a later relative of Wilbraham's remembers boiling a kettle up here for family picnics in the early nineteenth century. Arguments on rights and quarrying then took place seemingly endlessly until finally the National Trust took it over in 1937.

A camp meeting here on 31 May 1807 resulted in the founding of the Primitive Methodists, a breakaway from mainstream Methodism that wanted a back-to-basics return to Wesleyan ideals. Women evangelists were encouraged, and many Primitives later became trade union leaders. Founded by Hugh Bourne and William Clowes, Mow Cop evolved into a centre of religious revival, a movement culminating in 1,200 chapels and a 1907 centenary preach-in that saw 100,000 faithful gathering around the castle. In 1937 the stray sheep Primitives were brought back into the prevailing not-so-primitive fold, the only reminder now of their existence in the name high on the walls of often lonely chapels.

HORTON TOWER, DORSET

I first saw Horton Tower in a few frames of 70mm film, a location put to use as an illegal cockfighting den in John Schlesinger's 1967 *Far From The Madding Crowd*. It made me want to go south to see it for myself, this brick giant built by Humphrey Sturt in the 1760s as a possible observatory for him to study the heavens over East Dorset. It is far more likely that the tower was used as a vantage point to watch the progress of the local hunt rather than any eighteenth-century interstellar movement. More certainly, it started my passion for such things.

I don't think there's anything quite like the 140-foot-high Horton. A six-storey hexagon, flanked with three-quarter round turrets topped-out like mustard pots, squashing classical pediments between them. I first saw it on a rainy Easter Monday in 1968, probably hoping there would be a something leftover from the filming – discarded location catering coffee cups, Terence Stamp's cigarette butts, that sort of thing. There wasn't. But I could get inside, to look up through the now floorless interior to see the odd pigeon fluttering in and out of the window openings. The best story is probably the most recent, in that a mobile phone company has completely restored the tower and placed their transmission gubbins very sensitively so that they blend with the architecture and brickwork. So at last, after 240 years, Horton Tower really does reach out to the Dorset heavens.

KEW GARDENS PAGODA, LONDON

Princess Augusta, the Dowager Princess of Wales and mother of George III, was presented with this superb example of eighteenth-century *chinoiserie* as a surprise in 1762. Imagine trying to keep it a secret. When Horace Walpole saw it rising above the trees from his equally extravagant Strawberry Hill he was appalled, and said that '…in a fortnight you will be able to see it from Yorkshire'. At 163 feet high with ten storeys it is indeed tall, even for the time. Each storey is a foot less in overall width to give the tapering that makes the tower seem even higher. Designed by William Chambers, there were originally iron dragons enamelled in coloured glass snorting around each roof line, every creature with a bell in its mouth. Imagine that; walking through the gardens and hearing chimes sounding out over the trees and sunlight flashing off the gilded pinnacle. The slate roofs and dragons were removed to pay off George IV's debts.

Decimus Burton, busy with the glass houses nearby in the mid-nineteenth century, offered to put them back, but the cost was prohibitive. Maybe now someone should get the Ministry of Defence to put their hands in their serge trouser pockets. In the Second World War holes were made in each floor so that bomb boffins could test the aerodynamics of their prototypes by dropping them the full height of the tower's interior.

LEITH HILL, SURREY

I promise you won't find a better view in south east England. South of Dorking, this is the highest point, 965 feet, but brought up to the 1,000 feet mark by Richard Hull with this tower in 1765-66. He called it 'Prospect House' and at only twenty six miles from London there was a time when you could stand up here and count the spires of the capital's churches. If you were lucky you could even get a glimpse of the sea between Brighton and Worthing through a dip of the South Downs at Shoreham Gap. Hull lived at nearby Leith Hill Place, later to be the home of composer Ralph Vaughan Williams, and asked to be buried underneath his tower. On his death in 1772 it was ransacked of its interior furnishings and after falling into ruin filled with rubble and concrete. In 1864 a Mr Evelyn of Wotton House bypassed the interior with a stair turret on the corner in order for access to be once again reached to the viewing platform. By the early twentieth century the tower was a popular alternative to its neighbour Box Hill as a day out for Londoners. Eric Parker was writing of it in his *Highways and Byways in Surrey*, and a girl was up here selling tea and melons. In 1984 the National Trust fully restored the tower, removing all the debris and making safe the ascent.

Coming up here involves a tough steep climb up through the woods that will make you wish there was still a big juicy melon waiting for you at the summit. But it's worth it, particularly in May with the slopes hazy with bluebells and cuckoos calling out from the treetops. To the north the view extends over a patchwork of fields to the North Downs and beyond, to the south over the Sussex Weald, a landscape apparently so dense with trees that it comes as a surprise to unexpectedly see aeroplanes taking off into the blue from Gatwick.

ALFRED'S TOWER, SOMERSET

Out on the fringes of the Stourhead estate, with its temples, grottos and nymphs gathering to make a Poussin landscape, is a triangular brick tower on Kingsettle Hill. Now only just inside Somerset, this is thought to be the spot where King Alfred raised his standard prior to giving the Danes a good seeing-to in 879. The 160-foot-high tower was erected in 1772, not only in commemoration of this, but also to mark the end of the Seven Years War against France and, belatedly, the accession of George III. It is certainly deeply impressive, and one of the things I love about it is the fact that one comes upon it slowly. Even with its great height, Alfred's Tower isn't one of those monuments you casually see from all directions on your approach. You discover it by travelling a little over two miles north westwards from Stourton, following the signs but seeing no sign of it until eventually you emerge from under the trees and walk out onto the greensward. And suddenly there it is, towering against the light.

Designed by Henry Flitcroft for his Stourhead client banker Henry Hoare in 1765, it uses approximately 1.2 million bricks and cost Hoare £5-6,000. One of the three round projections on the corners contains a staircase that gives access to the top. After 205 steps you are 950 feet above sea level, and from here you can either gaze down into the depths of the hollow interior, or out across the more interesting (and obligatory) vistas of three counties: Wiltshire, Dorset and Somerset. At one time, it is said, these three counties met at this spot.

WIMPOLE HALL, CAMBRIDGESHIRE

'...I know these works are an Amusement to you'. So wrote Lord Lyttelton to Sanderson Miller on behalf of his pal Lord Hardwicke at Wimpole Hall. Miller was in great demand, seemingly falling over himself to erect fashionable sham ruins in every landscaped park he came across. Lyttleton had him put up a castle on his Hagley Hall estate in 1747-8, and as a result of his introduction to Hardwicke this *faux* castle was created 'at a proper distance from his house'. This was the whole point, to have a conversation eye-catcher that could be remarked upon over breakfast, or visited on post-luncheon strolls across the park. Looking straight through the house from the front door it's the first thing you see, on an alignment that reaches out from both sides of the Hall to ancient and artificial barrows in the distance.

Country gentleman Sanderson Miller rapidly drew sketches, including representations of the stand of firs that were requested as a backdrop to the ruin. These things were taken very seriously by wealthy clients, and in Hardwicke's case his castle was very likely meant to be loaded with expressions of his political beliefs. Construction started in 1767, but not before Miller had gone mad. It was completed by landscape gardener Capability Brown and architect James Essex, but Lady Hardwicke thought it didn't look ruinous enough. She should see it now. Time has done what it always does, fulfilling the promises that only decades of standing about neglected in all weathers can achieve, haunted now by pigeons posing ecclesiastically in the window openings. Lady Hardwicke would have approved.

POWDERHAM BELVEDERE, DEVON

In 1392 Sir Philip Courtenay started building Powderham Castle on the Exe Estuary south of Exeter, and in 1773 the second Viscount Courtenay fancied a gothic belvedere out in the parkland. Following the fashion for such things, (the similar Haldon Belvedere was built on a nearby hillside fifteen years later), the prospect couldn't have been better: sailing ships and pleasure yachts on the ever-widening Exe, sheep pastures and well-wooded slopes. Watercolourists and engravers got busy placing it in romanticised landscapes, and by 1835 architect Charles Fowler was instructed to convert the three-sided tower into two-storey accommodation.

In the next decade, observers on the tower would have witnessed the progress of Brunel's ill-fated South Devon Atmospheric Railway from Exeter to Dawlish making its way by the park at the side of the estuary. Two disastrous post-war fires nearly destroyed the Belvedere, but thankfully it's still here on its hillside. Look out for it on the right from a Newton Abbot bound train after you leave Exeter and before the line turns to run by the coast at Dawlish Warren.

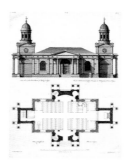

MISTLEY TOWERS, ESSEX

Mistley is next to Manningtree at the head of the Stour Estuary. If you're coming through from Harwich you will see big brick maltings on either side of the road, some converted to apartments, others still producing malt from local barley and ingredients for things like cake making. And then, at the bottom of the hill are these twin towers. At first glance they don't appear to make much sense, until you see that they sit in a churchyard and that there's something missing. And that's the main body of the church that once sat between the towers that were positioned at both the west and east ends.

In 1776 wealthy local politician and Paymaster to the Forces Richard Rigby brought in *über* architect Robert Adam to design a church that would fit in with his idea of Mistley becoming a new spa town. Adam produced these two pavilions as bookends to the surprisingly small church of St Mary the Virgin which disappeared in 1870 when a new church was built in Mistley. It all must have looked magnificent, a neoclassical church overlooking the estuary and doubtless looked out for by returning mariners to the quays at Manningtree and Mistley. Now, apart from one relatively small but busy quay, it seems that the two old Essex seaports turn their backs on their maritime heritage, with trees now obscuring the doubtless once welcome sight of the towers from the river.

KEPPEL'S COLUMN, SCHOLES, SOUTH YORKSHIRE

Just off the M1, Keppel's Column is found in a field on the edge of a little housing estate in Scholes near Rotherham. That bulge in the middle is called an 'entasis correction', introduced into columns where an optical illusion can make them appear to bow the other way. But because of a lack of funds the column isn't as high as it should be so it doesn't work, and there was also supposed to be a statue of Admiral Keppel on top which isn't there either. Keppel was a friend of the 2nd Marquess of Rockingham, Prime Minister for a short time and owner of racehorse Whistlejacket, the subject of Stubb's painting. He lived down the hill at Wentworth Woodhouse, and his architect, the incredibly prolific Jonathan Carr (1723-1807), undertook the commission. The Admiral had been very unfairly court martialled as a result of his ships falling apart at the Battle of Ushant against the French in 1778. The main reason being that Keppel's erstwhile compatriots had trousered the cash meant for repairs. Rockingham was desparate to support Keppel, and drew up plans for this column which commemorates his friend's aquittal.

Inside, a spiral staircase winds up through the core, but due to lack of repairs is closed to the public. I assume the metal trellis, fastened corset-like round the waist, is for retaining unpredictable brickwork. From the rudimentary platform at the top you would just about be able to see York Minster if you were lucky. The column is 115 feet high with 217 steps, at one point opening out into a small room with seats let into the column. Presumably to get your breath back.

LUTTRELL'S TOWER, CALSHOT, HAMPSHIRE

The Eaglehurst estate is difficult to find, off the road from Fawley to Calshot and embowered in trees. And unless you are a temporary resident in this remarkable Landmark Trust property, access is very private. But all is not lost, because the tower can be found by walking south along the beach at Calshot. Yews and ilex trees come right down to the Solent shore, and very soon a set of stone steps, designed by Portmeirion architect Sir Clough Williams-Ellis, can be seen descending grandly to the shingle. The tower itself is then revealed through a gap in the trees. Built in the 1780s for Temple Luttrell MP by Thomas Sandby, (the first Professor of Architecture at the Royal Academy), the tower is a very satisfying mix of Gothic and Regency styles, big sash windows opening out across either the lawns to Eaglehurst House or over the Solent to Cowes on the Isle of Wight. Perfect for high-class smuggling, a purpose for which it was undoubtedly put to use with a tunnel from the beach to the basement; where instead of brandy casks there now sits a ping-pong table.

What other purposes this tower must have seen. Queen Victoria nearly bought it, and we know that Marconi utilised its position when perfecting wireless transmissions in 1912. Surely it must have also been used as a vantage point to observe the Schneider Trophy races of 1931, when the air speed record of 407.5 mph was achieved here by Flight-Lieutenant George Stainforth on 29 September with the Vickers Supermarine seaplane S.6b. Perhaps a Royal Aero Club observer sat up here on a canvas chair – binoculars, cameras and cigarettes to hand as the seaplane was carefully towed out into the Solent on her pontoon.

BELLEVUE TOWER, BRININGHAM, NORFOLK

One mile north of Melton Constable Hall is this curious tower, out in the fields near the village of Briningham. It started life in 1721 as a smock windmill, and you can still see the octagonal base with its chamfered corners. Once part of the Melton estate, in 1781 the fourth Baronet Sir Edward Astley removed the wooden structure of the mill and built a prospect tower in pale orange brick. In the same year Armstrong noted in his *History and Antiquities of the County of Norfolk:* 'the tower, now called Belle-View ... is commodiously fitted up; the apartments and furniture elegant and the look-out at the top affords a prospect of sea and land twenty five miles each way'. It was restored in 1980-2 and is private.

The observatory at the top doesn't look particularly eighteenth-century, and that drainpipe doesn't help, but enough of the original is here on one of Norfolk's rare moments of rising appreciably above sea level. No doubt it was an ideal spot to watch location catering caravans and generators arriving at the Hall and its environs for Joseph Losey's beautifully atmospheric film *The Go-Between* (1971).

BRIZLEE TOWER, ALNWICK, NORTHUMBERLAND

A Latin inscription on the Brizlee Tower says 'Look around! I have measured out all these things; they are my orders, it is my planting; many of these trees have even been planted by my hand'. The very proud exclaimer was the 1st Duke of Northumberland, a compulsive arboralist who had this elaborately ornamental tower erected in 1781 as the crowning glory to his works on the Hulne Park estate west of Alnwick, where his castle dominates the north of the town. The architect was probably John Adam, although the Duke himself has been credited. The 78-foot-high hexagonal tower can be seen for a considerable distance, but the approach was carefully worked-out so that it is revealed in truly dramatic fashion as one walks up through the trees on Brizlee Hill.

The tower is built in six stages, with a verandah above the pointed gothic entrances and a vertiginous balcony below the final stage which supports a cast iron fire basket. This gives the tower what Pevsner calls '…a most curious outline'. What a sight this would have been if used, roaring flames reaching up above the dark trees. Except there are no existing records to say it was ever lit. However, local man John Common did do a headstand on it in 1868. The tower developed problems with rusting ironwork and the inevitable water penetration rendered the stonework unsafe. All has now been restored to its former glory, with works co-ordinated by Robin Kent Architectural Conservation. I wonder if they left a bit of Latin somewhere.

SEVERNDROOG CASTLE, LONDON

There's nothing new in trying to keep pirates' hands off commercial shipping. The East India Company were getting fed up with them, and on the 2 April 1755 sent their marine strong arm in under their Commodore and Commander-in-Chief William James, who attacked and captured a pirate stronghold off the coast of Malabar at Severndroog. James received a baronetcy in 1778 but died of a stroke in 1783 during the celebrations attending his only daughter's marriage. The next year his grief-stricken widow built this memorial to her husband, a three-sided tower in Castle Wood, just off the old Dover Road at Shooter's Hill.

In 1797 the tower was used as a triangulation point for linking England and France with a Royal Society theodolite, by 1847 it came under threat because someone wanted to put a 10,000 slot catacomb cemetery under the hill, and the Second World War saw observers up here plotting incoming Dornier bombers droning their way up the Thames Estuary. In 2004 it became a contender in BBC2's *Restoration* series, when architect Ptolemy Dean, on hearing its history, thought of it as 'a love erection; a great big brick thing rising up on the landscape' and his companion, surveyor Marianne Suhr, said 'I don't think you can say that Ptol'. But it was too late. It also didn't win, but at the time of writing has just been awarded a Heritage Lottery grant of a half-a-million towards finally restoring it to its former glory. Once again Londoners will be able to have far-reaching views over their city and the surrounding suburbia.

OLD JOHN, LEICESTERSHIRE

My very first folly tower, Old John sits on the highest point (700 feet) in Bradgate Park, 828 acres given to the people of Leicester and Leicestershire by Charles Bennion in 1928. It always reminded me of my school Coronation mug, but made out of the local igneous rocks. Bradgate Park has never been landscaped, and remains a very rare example of an untouched medieval hunting ground where deer still graze under the trees. Surrounded by a stone wall four-and-a-half miles long, at its heart is Bradgate House, one of the earliest unfortified houses. Now a gaunt red brick ruin, this was home to the unfortunate Lady Jane Grey who lost her head to the political machinations of her age after being queen for just nine days. Tradition has it that the parkland oaks were pollarded in remembrance of her ghastly fate.

The tower was created from a windmill by the 5th Earl of Stamford in 1786 as a memorial to Old John, the miller. When a coming-of-age celebratory bonfire was lit in the park, someone thought it a good idea to have a flagpole at the heart of the flames, and when it finally toppled over it felled poor John. The eighteenth century was not overly exercised with health and safety regs. Old John would have been used as a prospect tower to follow hunts, and when the Quorn met in the park it came into its own as a refreshment stop.

HALDON BELVEDERE, DEVON

Find your way to Exeter Racecourse and you'll see a sign for the Haldon Belvedere. If you're not careful it's very easy to miss it in the bower of trees on the right hand side of the road, but park in the space just before it and follow the path into the woods. The woodland walk takes you over a bridge and then the white turrets will come into view.

The triangular Haldon Belvedere arrived on this hilltop in 1788, built by Sir Robert Palk, a past Governor of Madras. Dedicated to his friend Major General Stringer Lawrence, founder of the Indian Army, the three-sided tower made a focal point on Palk's vast Devon estates and is also known as 'Lawrence Castle'. King George III came up here and, like many high points in the south of England, was probably used by Marconi for early wireless transmissions. The Devon Historical Buildings Trust renovated the tower in 1994, and it has now become, naturally, a wedding cake-like wedding venue. The top floor is available for short lets, the apartment giving views over to the Exe Estuary, Exeter, the South Hams and Exmoor. If it's a particularly clear day they say you can see the Isles of Portland and Purbeck; maybe even Wales.

STRATTON'S FOLLY
LITTLE BERKHAMPSTEAD, HERTFORDSHIRE

Tucked away in a Hertfordshire village, this embattled red brick tower
was built in 1789 by Admiral John Stratton. Rumour, that stalwart
recounter of tales, has it that Stratton erected it in order to view
shipping on the Thames. Even as the adventurous crow flies this is
getting on for nearly thirty miles, so one can safely say that this was a
somewhat over ambitious objective, even with the highest powered
telescope of the day. But there was once a library reached by 150 steps,
where perhaps the Admiral reclined with maritime books whilst looking
wistfully out across the countryside, wishing that the river and his
beloved ships were nearer. The tower is 100 feet high, a round tower on an
octagonal base that utilised bricks from a demolished house nearby, and
built close to the site of a former brewhouse.

Towers erected by individuals often have stories attached to them that
have the owners wanting to be able to see or watch over something
normally out of reach. It may be the thought of being able to keep an
eye on labourers in surrounding fields, to show off the extent of an estate
to admiring guests, to facilitate the following of a local hunt, or, more
romantically, to gaze at the final resting place of a loved one in a distant
churchyard. In the eighteenth century the new obsessions with science
meant that observatories were the latest must-have building needed to
bring one nearer to the heavens, and Stratton's is often referred to as
being constructed for just this purpose.

CHARBOROUGH, DORSET

Long associated with Thomas Hardy's novel *Two on a Tower*, this octagonal landmark rises above Charborough Park in east Dorset.

'Upon this object the eyes of lady and servant were bent. "Then there is no road leading near it?" she asked. "Nothing nearer than where we are now, my lady." "Then drive home," she said after a moment. And the carriage rolled on its way.'

So jealously guarded is the privacy of the estate, with its three-mile wall keeping ragamuffins and itinerant photographers at bay on the A31, the back lane between Winterbourne Zelston and Lytchett Matravers is about the nearest we can get without risking a shotgun expelling itself near our trousers. I should imagine. On a more recent visit I was amazed to be unable to see the tower over the treetops from the same place I'd photographed it a couple of years earlier. Surely its sylvan setting could not have grown to such a height in order to create its apparent disappearance.

The Charborough Park Tower was built in 1790 by a member of the Drax family (wasn't there a Bond villain called that?). As was often the case with this kind of thing it got struck by lightning, and was subsequently built even higher in 1840. Look out for the estate on the left of the main road between Wimborne Minster and Dorchester, with the equally remarkable Stag Gate near the village of Almer.

BROADWAY TOWER, WORCESTERSHIRE

How many times have we read 'From the top of this tower you can see five counties.'? Well, the Broadway Tower won't be left out. James Lees Milne reckoned you can see thirteen from the battlements of Broadway, James Wyatt's tower built in 1797 for the 7th Earl of Coventry. It only just sneaks into Worcestershire, so much of Gloucestershire can be seen. It should be possible to see Warwickshire, Northamptonshire, Oxfordshire, Monmouthshire, Herefordshire and, before we had to call it Avon, the northerly parts of Somerset. Wiltshire and Buckinghamshire are pushing it a bit, which still leaves three more to go. On an exceptionally clear day you might get Berkshire, Leicestershire and the pale mauve hills of Powys. But I've never been in south-west Leicestershire and thought 'Ooh look, there's Broadway Tower'. Still, it's an intriguing exercise to ponder on – just how far you're seeing from the top of this 1,024-foot-high hill.

Broadway Tower came into existence as a landmark for those staring out from Croome Court, just fourteen miles away to the west of Pershore. The Countess insisted a beacon be lit on the hill above the Cotswold town of Broadway to ensure the tower would be seen. She was right to. As the crow flies, Bredon Hill is between the two points. Wyatt brought together all the fashionable details: Norman round-headed windows, turrets, machiolation and battlements, and the tower is now the crowning glory of a country park, open all the year round. Come up here on a winter's afternoon as the last of the sun lights the southern slopes of the Malvern Hills and the floodplains of the River Severn.

BOURBON TOWER
STOWE, BUCKINGHAMSHIRE

What is this? A folly dedicated to the chocolate biscuit of the same name? With an over-size sample stuck on top? Sadly not. The Bourbon Tower was an early arrival in Stowe's procession of landscape buildings, originally known as the Keeper's Lodge and attributed to Vanbrugh. Built of ironstone out in the deer park, it must have acted as a visible deterrent to the ever-present poachers. An 1805 drawing shows that there was once a shallow conical roof rising up from above the Romanesque arcading, but the octagonal 'biscuit' was apparently added when the previously level ground around the tower was embanked in 1843. This provided additional fortifications (that included a nearby cannon and rifle range) so that the 2nd Duke could put it to use as the centrepiece for manoevres with his beloved Buckinghamshire Yeomanry, of which he was the commanding officer.

There is, fancifully enough, a very tenuous connection between the tower and the chocolate biscuit (introduced in 1910) in that both were named after the French Bourbon royal family. Exiled and living at Hartwell in the same county, Louis XVIII and his entourage visited Stowe and the tower was renamed in his honour. Seven of his relatives are said to have planted four clumps of eight oaks in the immediate vicinity of the tower, but one can imagine that the real work was done by numerous labourers running about with wheelbarrows whilst a band belted out *La Marseillaise.*

WATERLOO TOWER, FINEDON, NORTHAMPTONSHIRE

On a bend of the A510 between Finedon and Cranford is this round tower. It now looks out over the fields to some of the most appalling-looking wind turbines in the country, their giant blades scything through both the local wildlife and the biscuit-flavoured air emanating from the nearby Weetabix factory. Such is 'country' life in this part of Northamptonshire. It wasn't always so. General Charles Arbuthnot bought the local Woodford House estate in the early nineteenth century and erected the tower to celebrate his chum Wellington's victory at Waterloo in 1815. It is said that Wellington climbed up onto the walkway at the top and pointed out his military strategies to others by waving his stick at landmarks in the countryside below that happened to bear a resemblance to those of the Napoleonic battlefield.

Later in the same century the tower became an inn known as The Round House, a popular stop-off for the hounds meeting at Finedon Poplars. Later it also became a good congregating point for working men out for Sunday strolls from the surrounding villages and towns. Boot makers discussing soles and heels, furnace men getting hot under their collars. It naturally enough got very competitive, with sprinting, dog racing and marathon domino sessions. Gypsies who camped nearby rolled up their sleeves and the field opposite the inn became notorious as the scene of violent brawling and general mayhem. By 1895 these activities became formalised as the Victory Social Club, relocated to Finedon and called 'The Pam' after 'Panorama'.

WHITE NANCY, BOLLINGTON, CHESHIRE

Slightly out of kilter with the towers being shown here, where even a column makes it in if there are stairs to the top, (or at the very least a room inside), this curious cloche-shaped folly scrapes by because you *could* get inside it once, albeit just to sit at a round stone table on stone benches. Built to commemorate victory at the Battle of Waterloo, White Nancy arrived here courtesy of John Gaskell in 1817, apparently named after the lead horse that pulled the materials up here. White Nancy wasn't always white, the ball-finialled cone was built in sandstone rubble and only later rendered and painted. Once, unofficially and obviously, in flesh pink. I imagine it gets a coat of paint fairly regularly, as it provides an inviting surface for those with felt-tip pens itching in their pockets. Messages of a different kind were sent out from White Nancy in the mid-1940s when the Royal Signals Corps Trials Unit from Catterick drove a Bedford truck up here in order to erect a cathode ray transmitter. Receiving stations were positioned in relay on prominent hills until White Nancy was communicating with the south coast. I wish I'd known which way they came up here. This is a real heart-stopper of a climb up from Bollington, but when I finally staggered on to the summit I was met by two very cool girls who giggled in a most becoming manner at my perspiring countenance. 'I suppose you're going to tell me you came up the easy way,' I said between gasps for breath. 'Of course we have,' they replied, pointing back to a gently sloping footpath.

Local poet James Chatterton wrote 'milestone' poems about incidents in his life, and these are the first lines of one remembering his visit to White Nancy in 1919: *Once again I have called on Miss Nancy / Once again I have climbed up this hill / And although my age is oe'r eighty / I have the strength to climb it still.*

WATERLOO TOWER
BIRCHINGTON-ON-SEA, KENT

The simply extraordinary Waterloo Tower in Birchington-on-Sea sits out in the fields of Quex Park surrounded by dark yews. Only a mile or so from the sea, a red brick tower with four corner pavilions suddenly sprouts a cast-iron open weave spire balanced on the turrets. This almost science fiction wonder was modelled on the 1799 Faversham church spire, which adopted very similar buttresses in order to soften the blow should it fall into the town as a result of an explosion at the nearby gun-powder works. Built at the behest of John Powell Powell in 1819, the tower (constructed by the Quex Head Carpenter and Sandwich ironfounder William Mackney) contains a ring of twelve bells – surely one of the most unique places that bells are still rung in the country – and also triples-up as both a Battle of Waterloo commemoration and family mausoleum.

Archie Gordon, in his tall thin book *Towers*, remembers that '*During childhood holidays at Westgate it was possible once or twice to slope off alone on a bicycle to look at this pretty object. In my ignorance I thought it copied from the Eiffel Tower in Paris. I may even have toasted it in Eiffel Tower lemonade. I wonder if that is still made?*' I have to confess that on my first visit it wasn't the Eiffel Tower that came to mind so much as the red chequered rocket in Tintin's *Destination Moon*. But moon rocket or French Fancy, this is nevertheless a slightly eerie place to visit, away from the main house and certainly brooding a little in its enclave of trees motionless against the sky.

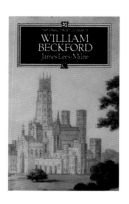

FONTHILL ABBEY, WILTSHIRE

Even though it no longer exists, this book would not be complete without mention of the extraordinary tower built up into the skies above William Beckford's Fonthill Abbey. Hence my highly improbable mock-up opposite. Even now, as I drive around the deep countryside south of Hindon, I expect to look up and see it still towering into the clouds, and then for it to slowly and silently fall down, a pall of dust billowing out over the trees. A small corner of the abbey is still up there, and the Fonthill Bishop gateway and twin pillars at the entrance to the estate, built by Beckford's father, still give out an echo of the curious activities that once took place here.

William Beckford (1760-1844) inherited his father's estate and fortune aged eleven, fell in love with Portugal, briefly got married and wrote one of the first gothic novels – *Vathek*. He sold his father's house and got James Wyatt to build a replacement on a neighbouring hill. His eccentricities included having a dwarf following him around, so his eye was probably taken off the ball when Wyatt and his contractor became negligent in the construction of the simply awesome 260-foot-high tower that promptly fell down in a raging gale. (It had to be in a storm didn't it?) Undeterred it was built again, but the estate was sold and in 1825 the tower collapsed again, this time the crumbling edifice chasing an aged retainer down a passageway in the Abbey. Beckford moved to Bath, where he couldn't resist erecting another tower, to the north of the town on Lansdown Hill where it thankfully still stays upright.

LANSDOWN TOWER, BATH

Once William Beckford had disposed of Fonthill in 1823, he took up residence in Bath. Ignoring for the most part the city's social elite, he nevertheless made a deep and lasting impression on his fellow citizens, going about in a curious cavalcade that included at least four grooms, the dwarf Perro, half-a-dozen dogs and the cadaverous Beckford himself on his grey Arab horse. He bought a house in Lansdown, (renaming it 'Baghdad'), and a patch of ground on the crest of Lansdown Hill. Where of course his thoughts turned to erecting yet another tower, and, rejecting the pitches by established architects, chose a design by Henry Goodridge, a 26-year-old developer from Bathwick. Commissioning the tower in 1825, it quickly started to rise above the downs north of Bath, with Beckford going about shouting 'Higher!' until a wood and cast iron belvedere based on the Grecian Temple of Lysicrates topped it out at 154 feet.

For such a man, steeped in eighteenth-century sensibilities, the tower was nonetheless very much of its time. Hung with scarlet curtains, the apartments provided storage for Beckford's paintings, cabinets, vases, candlesticks and jewels. From his eyrie he could sit and look westwards to the Bristol Channel and eastwards to his abandoned Fonthill. On Beckford's death in 1844 he was at first buried in Lyncombe Vale Cemetery, but four years later his daughter Susan bought back the tower and much of its garden for use as a cemetery. The tower was altered into a chapel and her father was duly brought up here to rest in the pink sarcophagus on the exact spot he had wished. Beckford is here still, among the trees and wildflowers that proliferate on this airy hilltop, in company with Goodridge, who also designed the cemetery entrance gate and superb Romanesque railings.

STEPPER POINT DAYMARK, CORNWALL

This could so easily be written-off as a redundant Cornish tin mine chimney, the vernacular style of which it so obviously borrows. This is the Stepper Point Daymark, built circa 1829 as a daylight warning to shipping negotiating the notorious waters of the Camel Estuary. Henry Price Rawlings wrote to the *Royal Cornwall Gazette* in December 1826, citing the fact that since 1800 no less than 96 vessels had been lost in the vicinity. Three years later the *Padstow Harbour Association for the Preservation of Life and Property from Shipwreck* was formed, and their first act was probably to find a shorter name. The chairman was Price Rawlings, under the patronage of the Reverend Charles Prideaux-Brune, and they made a start on making the maritime environment around Padstow less hazardous.

A lifeboat house was built in Hawkers Cove and capstans installed to aid navigation around the infamous Doom Bar across the Camel Estuary. The Daymark was built for £29, money being raised by offering voting rights in the Association – one vote for one guinea. It stands proud on the Point, 240 feet above sea level and 40 feet high, providing a mark now not just for sailors but for walkers on the coastal path, and is a welcome shelter in inclement weather. Just below is a watch house rebuilt from an empty shell that provides an excellent and much needed look-out for the local branch of the National Coastwatch Institution.

CLAVELL TOWER, KIMMERIDGE, DORSET

This extraordinary tower arrived here in the summer of 1830. In 1817, clergyman the Rev John Richards Clavell had, much to his surprise, inherited the Smedmore estate, acreage that contains the precipitous cliffs above Kimmeridge Bay. He built this tower using the rough stone from the immediate locality, together with fine Purbeck stone for the columns, parapets and decoration. So far, so good, except that these same cliffs are extremely friable, and after the tower had been neglected and fallen into ruin, so the cliff edge gradually came nearer and nearer. Until only 82 feet separated it from collapsing onto the rocky shore below.

The very difficult and thought-provoking decision was made to dismantle the tower stone by stone and re-erect it further back, and in 2006 work commenced with the careful numbering of every portion of the tower as it was taken down. I came up here during this process, and was intrigued to find that the wooden boxes used to store the stones were all marked 'Kodak'. The film processor's Hemel Hempstead works had recently closed, and I assumed the boxes once held thousands of those yellow plastic containers and were a job lot ideal for their new purpose. The original foundations were left exposed (above). Lead by the Landmark Trust, and with donations both very large and small, the work is now complete and the tower available for holidays. But be prepared for a 170-yard steep climb up from your car. Dogs are allowed – just be careful which direction you throw a stick.

KILSBY, NORTHAMPTONSHIRE

They reckon there's over a million bricks in it and they built a pub in Kilsby from what was left over. And this is only one of them. On both sides of the A5 south east of Kilsby these gargantuan red brick towers can be seen alone in the fields, and on an Ordnance Survey map you will see that they coincide with a tunnel on the main Euston to Birmingham railway. These are the Kilsby Tunnel ventilators, built by Robert Stephenson in 1835 to provide smoke outlets and ventilation for the line far below. The tunnel is 2,432 yards long, and at the time was the longest ever attempted. Stephenson discovered the same quicksand that had bedevilled the construction of the nearby canal in 1809, and the immense tunnel shafts (we only see the very top here) were the first things to be sunk, from whence the actual tunnel was bored out in two directions from each.

The whole enterprise quickly gained mythic status in the annals of engineering. The navvies employed to do the hard graft fought not only the unstable geology of the soil, but also themselves. There was always a fight going on, and three men lost their lives. Not from drunken fisticuffs, but from attempts to vault over the gaping holes before the castellated tops were built. Apart from The George public house in the village, built by moonlighting navvies, a nearby garden houses a contemporary miniature stone model of one of the tunnel entrances.

Tunnel ventilators have always fascinated me, perhaps because as a child I loved standing in the fields waiting for periodic billows of white exhaust smoke to suddenly rise up into the air, sometimes without even hearing the sound of steam trains rushing through in the dark below.

HADLOW TOWER, KENT

Walter Barton May built this octagonal gothic tower as the finishing touch to Hadlow Castle in the 1840s. Once again, the reasons for its construction vary, including the one about Walter wanting to see shipping in the English Channel. Most persistent is the story that the tower was meant to lure back Walter's wife, who had run off with a local farmer. Credence is given to this tale because it is reported that he wished for the tower to be seen by her wherever she roamed in the countryside. A preposterous erection indeed.

The tower is now 170 feet high, a top lantern and pinnacles being removed for safety reasons in 1996. The design was by George Leadwell Taylor, and apparently influenced by Beckford's tower at Fonthill Abbey. One hopes he used a more substantial cement. Full restoration is badly needed, but wrangles between the local council and changing owners delayed progress somewhat until a compulsory purchase order was issued. Work is now further hampered by the discovery that peregrine falcons are nesting there in truly gothic splendour. On my arrival here I met a Hadlow chap by the adjoining churchyard (where Walter was supposed to be buried sitting upright in a mausoleum – he isn't) who told me he thought the gothic interior had recently been put to exotic use to make porn films. We both looked up at the tower, lost in thought for a few moments.

BISHOP'S TOWER, OFFWELL, DEVON

In the early nineteenth century Bishop Edward Coplestone, formerly Provost of Oriel College, Oxford, was made Bishop of Llandaff in Wales. The unlikely story goes that he thought that if he built a tower high enough to be able to view his new Diocese from this Devon high point, he wouldn't have to actually go there. What Llandaff thought about this has been very difficult to ascertain, and of course, like so many towers, the potential field of vision was wildly exaggerated.

Coplestone was born in Offwell, a village two-and-a-half miles south east of Honiton, and built the 80-foot-high tower in 1843. The tower is now in the gardens of a private house, with its own Devon-style signpost on the crossroads opposite, and its fancy wrought-iron railings appearing to have Christmas decorations permanently attached to them. Which I think is a very sound idea – you wouldn't want to be hanging off parapets like these every December. Although I expect you ignore the traditional Yuletide custom that at least one fairy light bulb will have invariably failed.

HARDY'S MONUMENT, DORSET

This vast Portland stone chimney on Black Down commemorates Rear Admiral Sir Thomas Masterman Hardy, friend and embracer of Nelson on HMS *Victory* at the Battle of Trafalgar in 1805. He was no relation to his namesake, the Wessex author, but did have a brief walk-on part in the latter's *The Trumpet Major*. Hardy's country home was at the foot of Black Down in Portesham, known at the time as Pos'ham, and he set great store on victualling his ships with Dorset ale.

Designed by the remarkable-sounding Arthur Dyke Acland-Troyte, the 70-foot-high monument was erected by public subscription in 1844. The foundation stone was laid by Hardy's daughters on the 39th anniversary of the Battle of Trafalgar, on a spot where beacons would have been lit had there been a Napoleonic invasion. The views are, of course, exceptional. Eastwards over Martinstown to Dorchester, south eastwards to Weymouth and the Isle of Portland, south to Chesil Beach. And they say if you can see Hardy's Monument from a distance it's going to rain, if you can't see it it's already raining. Only the latter is true in my limited experience. But foul weather or not, film director Tony Richardson used the trackways through the gorse up here to shoot memorable scenes for his hugely popular 1963 film *Tom Jones*.

SOMERSET TOWER, GLOUCESTERSHIRE

Hawkesbury Upton lies in lonely country between Wotton-under-Edge and Chipping Sodbury in Gloucestershire. A turning off the Bath road at the junction with the Fosse Way takes you up through the village, where the Beaufort Arms pays obeisance to the Beauforts of nearby Badminton. At the top end of the village the ground falls sharply away down through the trees, the Cotswold escarpment merging into the flatlands that presage the Severn estuary to the west. It is here that you will find the Somerset Tower amongst the trees, in its own walled garden that includes a single storey custodian's cottage. At around 100 feet tall, this is the 1846 monument to General Lord Edward Somerset, who died just four years previously. The slender tapering column, designed by Lewis Vulliamy, has a big coat-of-arms on one side, a pedimented entrance and curious strapwork on the pyramidal roof that look like looping snakes. The narrow balcony and ineffectual-looking railings are guaranteed to produce sweaty palms I should think.

Robert Edward Henry Somerset was the son of the 5th Duke of Beaufort and a renowned and much decorated soldier. He served in the Napoleonic Wars, commanding his regiment at Talavera, Buçaco and Salamanca until taking on Milhaud's cuirassiers in a celebrated and successful charge with his Household Cavalry Brigade during the Battle of Waterloo in 1815. At various times he was MP for Monmouth, Gloucestershire and Cirencester.

GRIMSBY DOCK TOWER, NORTH EAST LINCOLNSHIRE

You can't miss this 309-foot-high red brick tower when you arrive in Grimsby. Dominating the docks, it's based on Siena's Palazzo Pubblico and designed by James William Wild. Queen Victoria opened it in 1854, and graciously gave her husband Prince Albert and the Princess Royal permission to ascend in the lift so that they could look down on the Humber Estuary and Cleethorpes. The Dock Tower was built to house hydraulic equipment that opened and closed lock gates, operate fifteen cranes and provide fresh water to ships and local docks housing. The engineer for the hydraulics was William Armstrong, who pioneered the use of water pressure for operating a crane on Newcastle docks in 1846.

The Dock Tower water tank is perched 200 feet up and held 30,000 gallons, the extreme height being deemed necessary to create sufficient pressure for the hydraulics. One million bricks were made from clay excavated on nearby marshes, and water draining into the foundations was mopped-up by bales of wool. The hydraulic lift is no longer in use, so a spiral staircase has to be used to climb up. Intrepid sportsmen have done this in order to abseil down the tower for charity, and such is its fame an oddly-proportioned version appears on a Cleethorpes Crazy Golf course (above), and there's one made of Lego in Legoland.

BULL'S TOWER, ESSEX

There aren't many towers in Essex, and those that are can be tricky to find. Pentlow Tower is tucked-up in the north east corner of the county just to the south of the River Stour, and is really only visible from a distance. Which means staring at it over flat fields of sugar beet. This red brick polygonal tower stands in the grounds of the old rectory in Pentlow, and was erected in 1859 by the Rev Edward Bull as a memorial to his parents. Apparently the Reverend gave the villagers a choice as to what to build. He asked them if it should be a row of cottages (sounds good), a drinking water well (mmm, even better). Presumably he whispered the first two options and then cleared his throat and said loudly 'Or a tall tower in my garden'. We assume that the good folk of Pentlow didn't want to upset their rector so went for the tower option. I hope he gave them free and unhindered access so that they could climb up and stare down at their sugar beet whenever they felt like it.

I also hope the good rector didn't get his parishioners to contribute to his fancy via the collection plate. I was amazed to find that the 1857 Scrabo Tower above Strangford Lough in County Down was erected by the grateful tenants of the third Marquess of Londonderry as a big (in fact bloody enormous) monument to him because he helped them out during the potato famine. For what it cost they could all have had cottage pies for life.

EAST CRANMORE, SOMERSET

East Cranmore Tower sits enclosed in beeches and firs, 919 feet above sea level between Shepton Mallet and Frome. A tall 1862 edifice with Italianate windows and jutting balconies, topped-out with a restored lead roof and pinnacle. It was constructed for Sir Richard Paget by Thomas Henry Wyatt, and although now private the little cottage at its side was once a very welcome tearoom in the 1930s. The Second World War saw the tower pressed into service by both the Home Guard and the Signal Corps, and is now once again open to the public, with access much improved with a new timber staircase.

Progress up to the tower can be slow and difficult. A path (incidentally crossing the course of a Roman Road) is clearly marked on the map, but I still found it remarkably easy to sink up to my knees in mud. The final approach was slightly forbidding, and a ghostly flapping glimpsed through the undergrowth turned out to be a line of washing at the base of the tower. The crowding round of the trees at least obscures to a degree the impact of the ubiquitous communications masts that share the hill, the highest point on the Mendip Way.

GUMLEY, LEICESTERSHIRE

Gumley is a village just across the fields from the famous staircase of
canal locks at Foxton. Joseph Cradock, an active promoter of the canal
and pal of both Dr Johnson and actor David Garrick, built the Hall here
in 1764. Two hundred years later it had gone, leaving just pleasant
woods, a lake, and the 1869 stables with its red brick clocktower. Built by
Hall resident Captain Whitmore, it looks like an Italian campanile, with
a Latin inscription – *Incorrupta Fides* (uncorrupted faith) – and the
obligatory weathervane dated 1870. The Murray Smiths took over the
Hall in 1897 until 1940, and were very active members of the Fernie
Hunt, founded in 1919. In October the hunt still has its first meet of the
season here, and it's easy to imagine the tower being used as a look-out to
watch progress over the surrounding pastures.

My brother had a paper round in Gumley, and early one very foggy
December morning arrived here in the dark to find a huge star in the
heavens above the village. He told me that he fell to his knees in awe,
thinking it was the Second Coming, but was mightily relieved (he still
had half the round to do) to realise that the heavenly body was in fact a
big Christmas decoration high above the stables, shining out above the
low-lying fog that had very effectively hidden the rest of the tower.

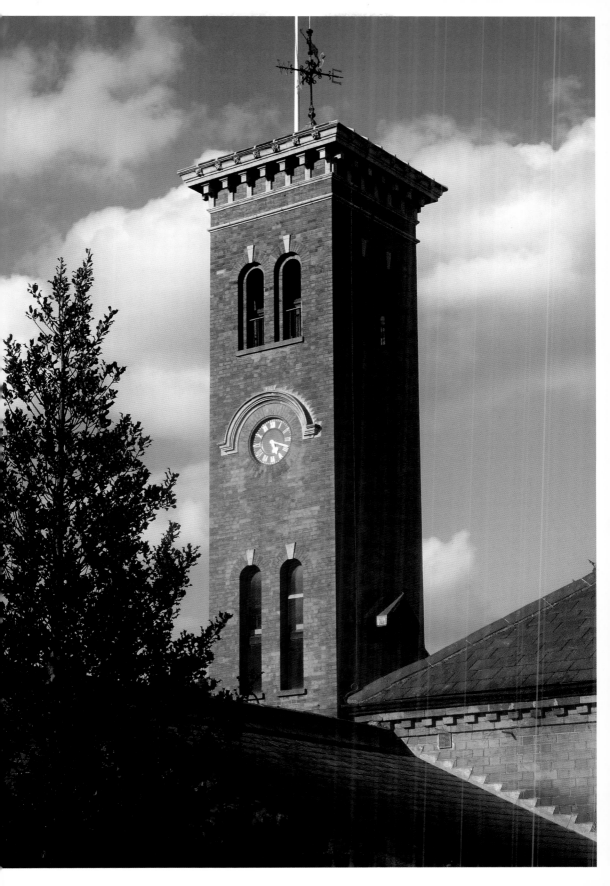

FARLEY MOUNT, HAMPSHIRE

A chalk trackway, a white pyramid, a dead horse. The track looks as if it was once used to connect Winchester with Romsey, a diversion off the Roman road to Salisbury, and at the top of Mount Hill is this slender white pyramid with a tiled porch on each side. Three of them blind, one opening into a tiny room. The views are magnificent, right down to Portsmouth, the reason it's here utterly bizarre. It records the leap a foxhunting horse made in September 1733 into a 25-foot-deep chalk pit with the owner, Paulet St John, still on its back. Both survived, and the deeply impressed huntsman went on to ride the same horse in the Hunter's Plate on Worthy Down in 1734. He won, his mount by now re-named 'Beware Chalk Pit'.

In 1740 the horse was buried here and a monument built on the mound. It's not exactly certain that this is the original; restoration was carried out in 1870 by the Rt Hon Sir William Heathcote and what we see today would appear to be different from a print made around 1860. Even more curious is the re-telling of the story on a Brooke Bond PG Tips card of the mid-1990s with a picture of a chimp doffing a top hat whilst riding past the monument.

WAINHOUSE TOWER, HALIFAX

After a Smoke Abatement Act came into force, John Edward Wainhouse (1817-83) needed a very large chimney to take the smoke away from his dye works in Washer Lane. But in 1874 he sold the works to his manager, who adamantly refused to have the uncompleted chimney in the deal. So Wainhouse brought in architect Richard Swarbrick Dugdale and spent £14,000 turning the smoke extractor into an immense 275-foot-high tower for himself. Gwyn Headley and Wim Meulenkamp, in their *Follies, Grottoes & Garden Buildings* said that 'the result of four years work is a belvedere tower by a medieval watch tower out of Chateau Chambord'.

The most persistent story, however, is the fact that Wainhouse had a big falling-out with Sir Harry Edwards, a fellow industrialist who was subjected to personal jibes and typical Victorian pamphleteering. Edwards appears to have largely ignored them, which must have wound Wainhouse up even more. The tower is supposed to have been used as a look-out post for Wainhouse to keep an eye on his enemy's activities down below, which seems to be a spectacular waste of time. Edwards apparently hated chimneys, so Wainhouse must have jumped at the chance to make his tower as noticeable as possible. It's a wonder he didn't keep white cattle and washing lines hung with white linen up here as well, two more of Edwards' phobias. An amateur radio station (call sign 2KD) broadcast from the tower during the First World War, and the belvedere was ideal as an ARP post in the Second.

ROUS LENCH, WORCESTERSHIRE

Rous Lench is one of a group of villages that owe their characteristic look to the Rev W. K. W. Chafy DD. FSA. The improving Reverend, who died in 1916, came to live in Rous Lench Court in 1876 and set about his alterations. The Court is now mainly the entrance buildings (above) to what was a much larger house that has all but disappeared, and it was to this property in 1647 that arrived one Richard Baxter, a puritan finding himself in royalist Worcestershire and a guest of Lady Rous, wife of Sir Thomas, 1st Baronet. During his stay he wrote his most famous work *The Saints' Everlasting Rest*, and the Rev Chafy was so enamoured of this that he built this Italianate campanile in his garden to celebrate the fact.

The 60-foot-high red brick tower, with its machicolations and stair turret, reminded Nikolaus Pevsner of 'an Italian Palazzo Pubblico', but to my mind there is a look of a Midland Railway water tower about it. Its position is now slightly emasculated by more recent houses and gardens, but it still looks magnificent against the brooding line of Scots pines.

Around here is what could be known as Archers' Country (I imagine), the vague setting for the fictional wireless serial. Indeed The Old Bull Inn in Inkberrow, just to the north of Rous Lench, is widely recognised as The Bull at Ambridge.

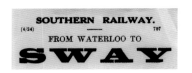

PETERSON'S FOLLY
SWAY, HAMPSHIRE

Andrew Peterson died in 1906, aged 93. His remains were interred in this tower, later to be removed by his family in the 1950s. It is unclear as to how Peterson got away with his monument: Trinity House complained about a proposed light on top being a distraction to shipping, others objected to the thought that it might make a good clocktower. Peterson was a judge who had spent his working life in Calcutta, returning to a cooler Hampshire with this retirement project in mind. He decided to use unreinforced concrete, apparently to prove a point, to make his mark with the 218-foot-high tower that remarkably has thirteen floors and eleven rooms.

Peterson got started in 1879 after building a small prototype that they say is still around somewhere, and utilised a workforce of 40 poor and unemployed local men. Many folly towers claimed the altruism of their builders in setting to work the disadvantaged, possibly as a distraction from their massive egos, more likely because it was cheap labour. But Peterson appeared to have genuine concern for his fellow man, and over five years the impossible structure slowly rose above the trees. It cost him over £30,000. A Mr Atlas bought it in the early 1970s for £2,700, and then came the violent storm of October 1987. Maintenance had not been a priority, and a couple of two hundredweight blocks alarmingly flew off during the night. That would normally have got Health & Safety foaming at the mouth and twitching to pull it down, but thankfully it prompted a full scale restoration costing £210,000, partly funded by English Heritage and the local council.

ABBERLEY CLOCK TOWER, WORCESTERSHIRE

This pink and buff stone clock tower is a real showstopper. Its height (161 feet) and comparative isolation on its Worcestershire hilltop between Droitwich and Tenbury give it the look of a giant grandfather clock left out on a lawn. Work commenced at Abberley Hall on 29 June 1883, and the topping-out occurred on 1 October the following year, the final bill coming out at £7,980.16s.6d. The clock room contained a carillon of 16 bells, and the sound was deflected down by one-and-a-quarter inch-thick plate glass louvres. Amazingly they have remained intact, only one has ever been broken – by a thunderbolt in 1969. The clock itself was provided by J. B. Joyce of Whitchurch and still marks the hours for the children and staff at the preparatory school below.

This preposterous erection was the idea of John Joseph Jones, who inherited the estate in 1880. One reason given for this flight of fancy, designed by architect J. P. St Aubyn, was that Jones wanted to regulate the activities of his large estate workforce by giving them the means to always know the time. But the most probable excuse for its appearance is that Jones wanted to literally put one over on his illustrious neighbours at nearby Witley Court, whose immense mansion (now an impeccable ruin) and landscaped park sprawls below. Presumably the female members of his household told him that if he was going to build such a thing in their garden then he could put a sewing room in the tower for them. And indeed that's what happened – it's behind the oriel window below the sun dial. Needles and thread gave way to binoculars and pencil stubs when the tower was occupied for the duration of the Second World War by the Home Guard, observing enemy aircraft approaching Birmingham.

BALKAN WATER TOWER, COLCHESTER, ESSEX

Although opened in 1883 as the Balkan Water Tower, this gigantic elephantine structure was quickly christened 'Jumbo' by the citizens of Colchester. The real Jumbo had just been controversially sold by London Zoo to showman Phineas T. Barnum, who paraded the incredibly large elephant around the USA and Canada until it was run over by a train. Even then Barnum cashed-in and paraded Jumbo's skeleton about on a railway truck. We use his name (probably a mis-hearing of the Swahili word for chief – *jambe*) for anything super-sized, but the Balkan Tower must have been amongst the first.

Designed by engineer Charles Clegg, it used 1.25 million bricks, 142 tons of iron and 369 tons of stone. The red-painted water tank once held 230,000 gallons of water, and even now this is the largest remaining Victorian water tower in Britain. And, very rarely, one of the few not to have been converted into a conversation piece home. Of course there have been numerous attempts to do just that here, developers falling over themselves to give penthouse views over Colchester. Why can't it be simply just left alone for what it is? I climbed up the central iron spiral staircase in 1988, past the scary dark depths of the thankfully empty tank to the roof and finally up into the cupola. A group of young people sat up there holding a prayer meeting. Wherever they are now, I want them to say one for Jumbo. A trust has been formed to do the right thing for this outstanding water tower, to save and maintain it as it is, a unique part of Colchester's civic heritage. Rather than yet another 'lifestyle' set of apartments and the obligatory restaurant. With sepia photographs on the wall of how it used to be, for you to glance at as you wait for your Jumbo steak.

LITTLESTONE WATER TOWER, KENT

This orange brick tower is an emphatic landmark in the flatlands of this corner of Kent, and only the Dungeness lighthouses and nuclear power station compete for attention. I first saw it as a child from the wonderful Romney, Hythe & Dymchurch Railway, as the small scale train approached New Romney station. It appeared as a grey silhouette on the horizon, looking slightly misshapen due to the suspended turret on the south east corner. It has fascinated me ever since, but only when collecting towers for this book did I finally track it down at the end of Madiera Drive and realise just how near the sea wall at Littlestone-on-Sea it is. Although now a residence, it must still act as a useful seamark.

Henry T. Tubbs was an entrepreneur who wanted to create a seaside resort on this stretch of coast, something to rival nearby Folkestone or Hastings. Starting with the basics he built this water tower in 1890 to service the hotels, terraces and parades of his vision, but the water was found to have an unhealthy salt content, so it was abandoned. In 1902 a new water tower was built at Dungeness that served a much wider area. Tubbs' seaside dream never saw the light of day shining up off the shingle, even his pier got built at Eastbourne instead. Today the only souvenirs of the venture are a row of somewhat ghostly tall houses facing out over the sea, incongruous without the trappings of a proper brass band playing promenade. Those circular recesses on the tower elevations must once have held clock faces; as it is the blank discs are perhaps a sad reminder of unfulfilled desires locked in time.

SHOOTER'S HILL WATER TOWER, LONDON

Some years ago, crossing Blackheath every night, I always looked out for the silhouette of this water tower on the horizon, a wonderful octagon of multi-coloured brick that stands 500 feet above sea level. Water companies in 1910 were never slow in self-advertisement, and this tower on Shooter's Hill was no exception. They spent £3,256 (around £185,000 now) for water to be pumped up here from chalk wells in Orpington, thence to fall by gravity down to a pumping station in Well Hall.

Although inevitably looked at by snake-eyed developers as prime real estate for non-affordable housing, the Shooter's Hill tower amazingly still remains as a receptacle for water, albeit with the obvious additions of mobile phone aerials. After I'd pressed the shutter a 'Community' Police Officer stepped out from behind that bus. He demanded to know what I was doing, in a voice that suggested that nobody in their right minds photographs water towers, and so, by default, I was a suspected terrorist on a recce for a bombing mission that would include all the other radio masts on the hill. Remembering a similar incident outside Bishopsgate police station, I got ready to be spreadeagled over the bonnet of a Met. unmarked car and have armed officers confiscate my camera so that they could all gather round to look at the pictures of other towers and a girl in a polka dot dress.

GOOLE COAL HOIST, EAST YORKSHIRE

Goole is full of idiosyncrasies. You only have to look at the two water towers (above), known locally as the Salt & Pepper Pots, to see that such things are taken very seriously in this inland port. The Victorian red brick tower with its giant ballcock shoved in the top was the town's water supplier until the growth in population required the concrete monster to be constructed next to it in 1926, at the time the largest ever built.

But round the corner on Aldam Dock is something else, the last surviving Goole coal hoist. Is it a tower? Not really, but that tapering turret at the top lets it into this book, and I just love it. Up until the mid-1980s coal was brought to Goole from the Yorkshire mines in strings of compartment boats that held 40 tons each and looked like floating railway trucks, pulled first by steam tugs and then diesel. An axe was kept handy in case one compartment sank and threatened to take the rest with it. Known as 'Tom Puddings' each compartment was separated from its neighbour and hoisted up this 90-foot-high tower and tipped forward so that the coal shot down a chute into a waiting freighter. Two blokes with shovels known as 'Spout Men' made sure all the coal was out. Designed by William Hamond Bartholomew (1831-1919), who also designed the Tom Puddings, five hoists saw service from 1863 to 1912, the No 4 hoist adding to the drama by being able to float about on the water to where it was required. The record for loading a ship with coal was reached in 1947 as 251 tons were loaded into the *Lady Sheila* in half-an-hour. She left on the same tide she came in on. The last hoist was used in 1985, and seen here is No 5, now a haunt for pigeons and a superb subject for photographers.

PRINCETHORPE, WARWICKSHIRE

The tower at Princethorpe is almost detached from the church of Our Lady of the Angels at its feet, and is certainly worthy of inclusion for its quite preposterous, almost fluorescing presence. It is one of those structures that one can't get out of one's mind, and I always look out for it across the fields as I drive up the hill opposite on the Fosse Way. Very early one autumn morning I was rewarded by the sight of it rising dramatically up out of the fog like a William Morris medieval fantasy.

It will come as no surprise that the architect was a member of the Pugin family – Peter Paul, son of Augustus Welby Northmore Pugin who believed the Gothic was the only true Christian architecture (classicism being pagan, obviously). Now Princethorpe College, an independent Catholic day school, the original buildings were built as St Mary's Priory for Benedictine nuns from Montargis who fled from the French Revolution. The new church was begun in 1897 and consecrated in 1901. Did ever a building so effectively dominate everything else around it?

FINEDON WATER TOWER, NORTHAMPTONSHIRE

Up on a ridge above the River Nene is this imposing example of
Edwardian waterworks engineering. All I know of the architect is that
his name was A. Cox, and the tower was part of a £13,000 project to
bring fresh water to the people of Finedon. The polychrome brick tower
was completed in 1904 at a cost of £1,500, and the sheer exuberance is so
impressive. The base of engineering blues so beloved of railway viaduct
builders, the barcodes of cream and orange brick, the *faux* Norman
castle machiolation and arcading. And a parapet that reminds me of
something by Voysey – perhaps the only industrial building he did –
Sanderson's wallpaper factory in Chiswick completed just two years
before.

New owners moved into part of it in 1980, and floor by floor they
converted the entire tower into a home. A real (and very expensive)
labour of love, but they are to be congratulated for retaining so many of
the original features, on the exterior at least. The water tank is still there,
although it was discovered not to have been drained and consequently
gallons of stagnant water had increased the problem of insidious damp.
More surprising, and indeed ironic considering the tower's purpose, was
the revelation that no mains water had ever been installed.

HOUSE IN THE CLOUDS, SUFFOLK

The coastal village of Thorpeness is so full of intriguing buildings it resembles a randomly put together Toytown. Houses that look like they've been made out of Bayko, cottages that look like pantiled barns and 1920s mock-Tudor everywhere. This is the dream village of Glencairn Stuart Ogilvie, who wanted to give families, and in particular the children, a sort of *Swallows & Amazons* experience, all big shorts, healthy eating and lots of contented pipe-smoking. Ogilvie wanted his holiday-makers '...*to experience life as it was when England was Merrie England*'.

His fantasy village needed a big water tower, and a 70-foot-high one was built in 1923 by Braithwaite Engineering. But how to disguise such an ugly erection that towered over the trees and held 50,000 gallons of water. (They brought the post mill opposite across from Aldringham to do the pumping.) With his architect F. Forbes Glennie and works manager H.G. Keep, Ogilvie came up with the idea of encasing the tank in a mock house. A 'House in the Clouds' as his first tenant Mrs Malcolm Mason immediately called it. Being a children's book writer she also went on about the real owners being fairies. In 1943 a Bofors anti-aircraft shell whizzed through the tank whilst two Miss Humphreys slept on undisturbed downstairs.

The tank was removed in 1979, cut up into manageable sections that were then lowered to the ground. So although the top was indeed once a fantastical piece of three dimensional *trompe l'oeil*, it is now a large room with outstanding views over the Suffolk coast and hinterland. And you can take your own holidays up here in the clouds – there are five bedrooms and three bathrooms on floors connected by 67 stairs. You will need telescopes, battered Arthur Ransome books and a 1925 Keep Fit manual.

CAMBRIDGE UNIVERSITY LIBRARY

If you think this looks like part of a 1930s power station, you'd be right. The designer was Giles Gilbert Scott, responsible for the look of the London Bankside and Battersea power stations and the irreplaceable red telephone box. Built in 1931-4, the tower has been the subject of much myth and legend, probably made-up by those using the academic facilities. The reference to it being called 'a magnificent erection' has been attributed to both Neville Chamberlain and King George V, and is alleged to be the inspiration for the *The Dark Tower*, an abandoned science fiction novel by C. S. Lewis.

For a long time its contents were obscure and uncatalogued, which led to rumours that the tower was stuffed full of pornography, but in 2006 a grant of half a million pounds meant that the shelves were investigated and dust blown from the volumes resting there. Remarkably, the content of the tower appears to be publications that the University at one time considered too low brow for inclusion in the main library. Innocent popular volumes of racy Victorian fiction with titles like *Tempted of The Devil*, *Only a Village Maiden* and *Love Affairs of A Curate*, but also first editions of Dickens, Conan Doyle and the Brontës were discovered amongst the mountains of ephemera that include trade pamphlets, photo albums, calendars and catalogues. A veritable tower of books; not a bad thing at all.

FARINGDON TOWER, OXFORDSHIRE

Lord Berners was one of the most brilliant stars in the firmament of English eccentrics. He had a clavichord in the back of his Rolls-Royce, dyed fantail doves in rainbow colours, kept a giraffe and when playing the piano supplemented his hands with his bottom. He was the model for Lord Merlin in Nancy Mitford's *The Pursuit of Love*. A man like this has to have a folly built, and the tower duly arrived on a hill above Faringdon in 1935, one of the last folly towers to be built. His great friends John and Penelope Betjeman were at the opening. It sits on Folly Hill, a landmark on the Oxford to Swindon road, and rises above a dark wood where in season foxgloves can also be seen reaching up to the light.

Berners wanted the gothic style, and was not pleased when he returned from Rome to find that his architect, Lord Gerald Wellesley, had gone for a classical tower. A gothic top was subsequently added. All involved hoped for apoplectic outrage from the locals and this was very swift in coming. A Miss Lobb complained, amongst other things, that the new tower was an invitation to would-be suicides. Berners promptly nailed up a notice: 'Members of the Public committing suicide from this tower do so at their own risk'. Lord Berners was also an artist, memorably designing the cover for the first Shell Guide to Wiltshire, and painted his folly on its tree-topped hill for a 1936 Shell lorry poster. Adding to the wonderful eccentricity of this place, a small but beautifully-lettered iron plaque is attached high on the northern wall, with the legend 'Please do not feed the giraffes', the plate 'supplied by my equine friend Moti' which was Penelope Betjeman's grey Arab stallion that Berners painted, along with the owner, in his drawing room.

LEWIS'S TOWER, LEICESTER

This tower is all that's left of Lewis's 1935-6 department store in Humberstone Gate in Leicester. I always thought the tower was the best bit anyway, even though Nicklaus Pevsner in his *Buildings of England: Leicestershire and Rutland* (1960) remarked that it was 'definitely not in a good taste, but by its very queerness and uncouthness an established landmark'. Funny, I thought he'd go for it. The architect was Gerald de Courcy Fraser, who designed Lewis's 1947 flagship store in their home town of Liverpool. Paul McCartney had a part-time job there, presumably before playing left-handed bass in the well-known combo.

I was dragged around the Leicester store many times as a child, (yawning in Household Goods, blushing in Lingerie), only cheering up when Santa appeared in his hardboard grotto at Christmas, dispensing razor-sharp tin toys. I honestly believed he arrived by landing his sleigh in a steeply-angled and abrupt stop on the tower roof, like a helicopter on a lighthouse pad. Later the tower was a *leitmotif* for us dermatologically challenged youths arriving to stare at girls on the perfume counters in their black uniforms. I never did find out what happened in the tower's glass eyrie, but one suspects it was ideal for firewatching in the Second World War, having a perfect view of surrounding rooftops in the city centre, and of my father running around next door on the roof of Boots the Chemists with a bucket of sand.

BALDERTON, NOTTINGHAMSHIRE

The imagination can run riot here at Balderton. A tower of such overpoweringly surreal proportions and colour, it looks dark and sinister even on a cloudless day. Backlit against a raging sunset it could provide a hellish image for a Dracula movie set in the 30s. In thankful reality it's a chimney, serving the Balderton Hospital that once gathered at its feet, part of a development started in 1936. Wartime halted construction, when the large Victorian house on the site was used by officers from Balderton airfield. Work recommenced in 1945, but it was not finally opened until 1957, by Minister of Health Enoch Powell. It was what we once called a mental hospital, and the tower dominated a laundry block that looked more like an engineering factory; an indicator of just how extensive the operation was here.

The chimney is still there, but the hospital has vanished, closed in 1993. Now it is surrounded by an estate of houses in the usual doubtful pastiches, where the view out of the window must seem as though a neighbour has planted a monstrous garden ornament. Big chimneys at hospitals often doubled-up as drying rooms for bedsheets, one very Gormenghast example once towered over the Leicester General Hospital, black smoke often seen pouring from its flue. My elder brothers gleefully told me this was where they incinerated amputated limbs, an image that subsequently haunted my childhood until the tower was demolished.

POST OFFICE TOWER, LONDON

The emblem of Prime Minister Harold Wilson's 'white heat of technology'; a tower to go with Mary Quant, early James Bond films, The Beatles and Antonioni's film *Blow-Up*. Up until the mid-1990s this was an official secret in a Fitzrovia back street west of Tottenham Court Road. A bit like those books with titles like 'Secret Britain', and road signs pointing to 'Secret Bunkers'; just how did they think we wouldn't notice a 620-foot-high tower? Particularly with a revolving restaurant on top that completed a circuit during the soup course. So secret it has only recently been allowed into our London street atlases, a giant symbol of its time. Away with party lines and press button A, we now speak to the world with microwave ovens strapped to steel and glass.

Previously, the GPO (as it then was), had to make do with a pylon on top of the Museum Telephone Exchange. (MUSeum – remember that?) And then plans were drawn-up by Eric Bedford and G. R. Yeats from the Ministry of Buildings and Works for the 1965 Post Office Tower. The restaurant didn't revolve for long, and in 1971 the IRA let a bomb off in the gents. Thankfully nobody was injured, just a security guard lifted up out of his chair, but in 1981 BT decided it didn't want us looking over London from its eyrie, so it was finally closed to the public who pay their imaginative bills. A secret no more, just another anonymous London address – 60 Cleveland Street, but it's worth craning your neck for when you next go looking for furniture on Tottenham Court Road.

BT LABORATORY, MARTLESHAM, SUFFOLK

Anyone who has ever driven to the Suffolk coast via the Orwell Bridge will recognise this extraordinary sight. This is BT's 'laboratory', built in the days when our beloved telephone company was emerging out of its GPO chrysalis. Gone were the bronze green telephone service vans with wooden ladders on the roof, on the way out were rows of girls with headphones on saying 'Putting you through now caller'. 'Laboratory' says it all really, men in white coats and goggles experimenting with coils of copper wire and resistors, talking in hushed whispers on Trimphones. It's that air of secrecy, like the impenetrable Post Office Tower in Fitzrovia, that there's stuff going on in hermetically-sealed offices that we mustn't know too much about. How I'd like it to be of course, is that when you finally get past a dozen security checkpoints and had your forehead barcoded, you find a long room with a boffin at each end shouting to each other down a line of string joining two empty Golden Syrup cans.

There has been experimentation going on here for some time. In 1917 the Royal Flying Corps turned up from Wiltshire, the remote heath an ideal place to mess about with doped-up canvas and wooden strutting. The Post Office bought part of the airfield in 1968, moving all the wire and white coats up from Dollis Hill. It must have been like an episode of the Avengers, locals falling silent when bespectacled sports-coated men came through the pub door. But what I really want to know, instead of making things up is, does that angled box on the tower turn round on the one underneath? It looks as if it should. Tannoys bursting into metallic life: 'Hold tight everyone, rotation starting now'.

RUSHMORE ESTATE, WILTSHIRE

Is this the last of the breed, or the start of a new era of folly building? Only time will tell, but here is something truly extraordinary for our age, precisely placed not only in line with King John's House on the Rushmore Estate, but also exactly on the border between the counties of Wiltshire and Dorset. William Gronow-Davis is the owner and folly lover, and originally O2 were going to use the 65-foot-high structure to house mobile phone masts. When they pulled out of the deal it left the tower useless, which of course made the building of it even more appealing.

The folly (at the time of writing without a definitive name) was designed by architects Walshe Associates and is in the style of an Indian Mogul gateway, a nod to the birthplace of Gronow-Davis. All it needs is a few vultures wheeling about above the five copper domes. The base is faced in limestone panels, the whole rendered in red ochre lime with white for the detailing. The effect is startling to say the least, isolated on the ridge between Farnham and Tollard Royal, and is probably the tallest of such things for a hundred years. Opinion is naturally divided between those who love it exactly for what it is (that's me then) and those who are repulsed by it, denouncing it in the usual resentful and envious terms of it being a waste of time and money. 'You could build a hospital for what it cost', that sort of thing. No you couldn't, and without the imaginatively eccentric visions of landowners and architects over the centuries like William Gronow-Davis, the English countryside would be much the poorer. If I had the wherewithal I'd build one. I know where it should be, I know what I want it to look like. And it wouldn't bother me in the slightest when someone came across it and said 'What a preposterous erection'.

ACKNOWLEDGEMENTS

Abberley Hall School, Stephen Allen, Kathy Ashley,
Nicky Balfour Penney, Lucy Bland, Broadway Country Park, Cambridge University,
Christopher Clark, Teresa Cox, Denny Einav, English Heritage, Rupert Farnsworth,
Jay Goldmark, Mike Goldmark, Richard & Jane Gregory, Elizabeth Huxtable,
Leigh Hooper, The Landmark Trust, Roger Porter, National Trust,
Princethorpe College, Quex Park, Biff Raven-Hill, Margaret Shepherd,
Vic Uttley, Philip Wilkinson.

Page 1: *Piers Plowman* William Langland, Penguin 1959 (trans: J.F. Goodridge)
Page 60: *Towers* Archie Gordon, David & Charles 1979
Page 90: *Follies, Grottoes & Garden Buildings* Gwyn Headley &
Wim Meulenkamp, Aurum 1999

The image on page 6 is a detail from the poster below:
Faringdon Folly *by Lord Berners, 1936. Courtesy of the Shell Art Collection.*

BIBLIOGRAPHY

John Betjeman and John Piper (eds), *Shell County Guides*, Faber & Faber
1934-84; Nikolaus Pevsner, *Buildings of England Series*, Penguin / Yale University Press,
1951 onwards; Philip Wilkinson and Peter Ashley, *The English Buildings Book*,
English Heritage, 2006; Archie Gordon, *Towers*, David & Charles, 1979; George Mott and
Sally Sample Aall, *Follies and Pleasure Pavilions* Pavilion, 1989; Gwyn Headley and
Wim Meulenkamp, *Follies, Grottoes & Garden Buildings*, Aurum, 1999;
Stuart Barton, *Monumental Follies* Lyle, 1972; Barbara Jones, *Follies & Grottoes*,
Constable, 1953; James Lees-Milne, *William Beckford*, Century, 1990;
Sue Clifford and Angela King, *England in Particular*, Hodder & Stoughton, 2006;
Derry Brabbs, *Landmark*, Weidenfeld & Nicolson, 1998; *The Landmark Trust Handbook*;
Hugh Casson (ed.) *Follies* (National Benzole Books), Chatto & Windus 1963

INDEX

Peter Ashley is the author and photographer of over twenty books,
including *Unmitigated England* and *More from Unmitigated England*.
Recent titles include *Cross Country* (2011) and
The Cigarette Papers (2012).

Thou shalt not remove
thy neighbour's landmark

DEUTERONOMY 19 v14